Where do animals live?

Bobbie Kalman

 Crabtree Publishing Company

www.crabtreebooks.com

Created by Bobbie Kalman

Author and Editor-in-Chief
Bobbie Kalman

Educational consultants
Reagan Miller
Joan King
Elaine Hurst

Editors
Joan King
Reagan Miller
Kathy Middleton

Proofreader
Crystal Sikkens

Photo research
Bobbie Kalman

Design
Bobbie Kalman
Katherine Berti

Production coordinator
Katherine Berti

Prepress technician
Katherine Berti

Photographs
BigStockPhoto: p. 5, 16 (bottom), 24 (top middle)
Creatas: p. 14, 24 (middle right)
Digital Vision: p. 15
Dreamstime: p. 23 (top right), 24 (top right)
 Shutterstock: cover, p. 1, 3, 4, 6, 7, 8, 9, 10, 11, 12, 13,
 16 (top), 17, 18, 19, 20, 21, 22, 23 (except top right),
 24 (except top middle, middle right, and top right)

Library and Archives Canada Cataloguing in Publication

Kalman, Bobbie, 1947-
  Where do animals live? / Bobbie Kalman.

(My world)
Includes index.
ISBN 978-0-7787-9449-3 (bound).--ISBN 978-0-7787-9493-6 (pbk.)

  1. Habitat (Ecology)--Juvenile literature.
I. Title. II. Series: My world (St. Catharines, Ont.)

QH541.14.K365 2010   j591.7   C2009-906108-2

Library of Congress Cataloging-in-Publication Data

Kalman, Bobbie.
  Where do animals live? / Bobbie Kalman.
    p. cm. -- (My world)
  Includes index.
  ISBN 978-0-7787-9493-6 (pbk. : alk. paper) -- ISBN 978-0-7787-9449-3
(reinforced library binding : alk. paper)
  1. Animals--Habitations--Juvenile literature. I. Title.

  QL756.K356 2010
  591.7--dc22

                                                       2009041230

Crabtree Publishing Company

Printed in Canada / 042018 / MQ20180319

www.crabtreebooks.com   1-800-387-7650

Published in Canada
Crabtree Publishing
616 Welland Ave.
St. Catharines, ON
L2M 5V6

Published in the United States
Crabtree Publishing
PMB 59051
350 Fifth Avenue, 59th Floor
New York, New York 10118

Published in the United Kingdom
Crabtree Publishing
Maritime House
Basin Road North, Hove
BN41 1WR

Published in Australia
Crabtree Publishing
3 Charles Street
Coburg North
VIC, 3058

What is in this book?

What is a habitat? 4

What do animals need? 6

A forest habitat 8

Dry deserts 10

Mountain habitats 12

Grassland homes 14

Very cold habitats 16

Wetland habitats 18

Ocean habitats 20

Which habitat is it? 22

Words to know and Index 24

What is a habitat?

A **habitat** is a place in nature.

Animals live in habitats.

Some habitats are on land.

Some habitats are in water.

Turtles live on land and in water.

A turtle has come out of the water
to warm its body in the sun.
The alligator is warming itself, too.

What do animals need?

To stay alive, animals need air, water, and food.

They need sunlight to keep them warm.

Animals find everything they need in their habitats.

Hummingbirds get food from the flowers in their habitats.

This crocodile caught a fish to eat in its habitat. The crocodile lives in water, but it comes up to breathe air above water.

A forest habitat

A **forest** is a habitat with many trees.

There are different kinds of forests.

This sloth lives in a **rain forest**.

A rain forest gets
a lot of rain.

sloth

This three-toed sloth eats and sleeps
in the trees of its rainforest habitat.

Dry deserts

Deserts are dry habitats.
They do not get much rain.
Plants called **cacti** grow
in some deserts.
Cacti have sharp **spines**.
Spines are like needles.

cacti

spines

Iguanas are lizards that live in deserts.

They eat cacti.

This iguana climbed on top of a cactus.

Mountain habitats

A **mountain** is tall, rocky land.

The top of a mountain is cold and windy.

The bottom of a mountain is warmer.

Mountain goats live at the tops of mountains in summer.

They live at the bottoms of mountains in winter.

They can find more food there in winter.

Mountain goats have **hoofs**.

The hoofs of these baby mountain goats help them climb up and down mountains.

Grassland homes

A **grassland** is a flat habitat that is covered with grasses and other plants. This grassland is called a **meadow**. Many red foxes live in meadows.

Foxes live in homes called **dens**.
The den of this red fox **kit**, or baby,
is inside a log in a meadow.

Very cold habitats

There are two very cold habitats on Earth. One is the Arctic. The other is Antarctica. The Arctic is at the top of Earth.

Arctic

Antarctica

Polar bears live in the Arctic.

Antarctica is at the bottom of Earth.

Penguins live in Antarctica.

Antarctica is the coldest place on Earth.

Wetland habitats

Many birds live in **wetland** habitats.
Wetlands are covered with water
most of the time.
These birds are
called spoonbills.
Spoonbills are
wading birds.
Wading birds
walk in water to find food.
They have long legs
and long **bills**.

bills

The bills of spoonbills are like spoons.

They help these birds scoop up food under water.

Long legs keep their bodies above water.

Ocean habitats

Many kinds of animals
live under water.

Some live in **ocean** habitats.

Oceans are big areas of salty water.

Many kinds of fish live in oceans.

Sharks live in oceans.

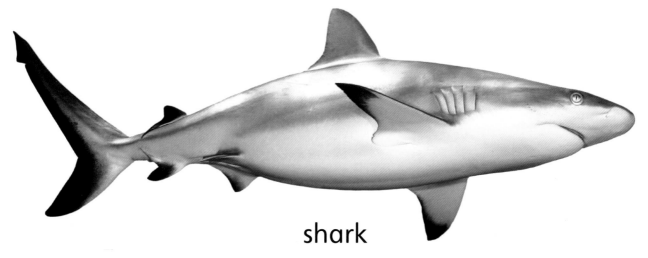

shark

Some sharks
are very big!

Which habitat is it?

Match the pictures to these habitat names.

1. wetland

2. desert

3. ocean

4. forest

5. mountain

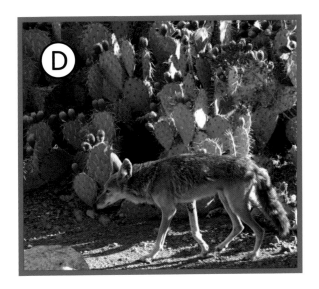

Answers

1-B

2-D

3-A

4-C

5-E

Words to know and Index

Antarctica
pages 16, 17

Arctic
page 16

deserts
pages 10–11, 22

food pages
6, 12, 18, 19

forests
pages 8–9, 22

grasslands
pages 14–15

mountains
pages 12–13, 22

oceans
pages 20–21, 22

wetlands
pages 18–19, 22